Cuisinart Convection Toaster Oven

Cookbook for Beginners

The Complete Guide of Cuisinart Convection Toaster Oven with Easy Tasty Recipes on A Budget for Anyone who want Improve Living

By Sharon Katie

Table of contents

Description

A bunch of delicious recipes that you can easily cook in your toaster oven, along with all the necessary tips and tricks!

The art of baking or cooking in an oven lies fairly on the quality and efficiency of the oven being used. Among all the toaster ovens out in the stores, Cuisinart Convection Toaster Oven is one of the most user-friendly ones. Today, toaster ovens are multifunctional and allow you to cook those recipes which you would've never imagined cooking in an oven. And this cookbook offers you a wide array of hacks to make your cooking and baking experience more adventurous.

Complete with 90 recipes, and step-by-step instructions on how to make them in your very own toaster oven, this book is for all those people who prefer hassle-free cooking.

It includes:

- Cuisinart Convection Toaster Oven 101
- What is Cuisinart Convection Toaster Oven
- Constructions and 15 Cooking Functions
- Basic Steps to Get Started
- Tips and Tricks of Usage, Cleaning, and Maintenance
- **90 Recipes You Can Try Out in Your Toaster Oven**

Buckle up - you're up for a pretty fun ride exploring loads of new recipes.

Introduction

Ovens have been a primary medium of cooking since the prehistoric times. In many archaeological sites, enclosed structures with grills and rods with sufficient heating space below have been discovered. Traces show that those might actually lead to the design of today's ovens and heating furnaces. All history aside, just think about how lucky you are to have some of the finest ovens at your reach now!

The oven industry is ruled by a number of manufacturers, who are striving to produce the smartest and most sustainable toaster ovens. Among them, Cuisinart has brought into the market a highly efficient toaster oven. It's built with all the newest features and specifications that you would be looking for in an ideal toaster oven.

One of the best features of a toaster oven is the low consumption of energy. This is because high-power ovens tend to take a toll on your bills. To resolve this problem, Cuisinart Convection Toaster Ovens have been designed to be highly energy-efficient. On top of that, you'll be able to bake and cook a wide array of dishes with this oven using its special set of options. The subsequent chapters will provide more information on this appliance.

Chapter 1: Cuisinart Convection Toaster Oven 101

This toaster oven is a highly versatile appliance for cooking and baking. It can make your favorite pizza and also satisfy your sweet tooth by baking brownies or cakes. People say that the quality of a toaster oven depends on the amount of money you're planning to invest in it. However, Cuisinart Convection Toaster Oven may not be one of the most high-end toaster ovens in the market, but in terms of functionality and performance, it will never disappoint its users.

What is the Cuisinart Convection Toaster Oven?

Cuisinart has been serving its customers for a long time with its trusted cooking and baking appliances. The various types of ovens, cooking ware, baking ware, grilling appliances, and many more make this manufacturer a top choice for customers. So, it comes as no surprise that Cuisinart produces some of the best quality toaster ovens in the market.

Imagine you woke up late from your sleep, and you have to reach your office in an hour. In such a short time, you'd have little to no time to prepare a proper breakfast. Don't worry! Cuisinart Convection Toaster Oven has got that covered. The highly versatile and rapid cooking system of the oven will get your breakfast prepared within minutes. Essentially, having a Cuisinart Convection Toaster Oven at your home will make your life much easier.

Construction and Cooking Functions

In terms of looks and design, Cuisinart Convection Toaster Oven does an outstanding job. It has a compact structure, allowing you to fit it at any spot in your kitchen conveniently. The toaster oven boasts a whole lot of new preset functions and cooking options, which will enable you to cook nearly everything you wish to cook.

Equipped with a 175W heating power, it is able to show amazing results in the shortest time possible.

Many tend to be confused about the settings, which can often result in burnt or uncooked food. With this oven, you can say goodbye to such issues, it sports a fancy digital display that will show the timer options, cooking options, temperature, and more. The interior of the toaster oven features a nonstick surface to prevent any messes while baking or cooking. To maintain a standard level of durability and robustness, it is fully constructed using stainless steel.

A key feature of this oven is its 15 distinct cooking functions. Let's have a brief look at how these functions can enhance your cooking experience.

1. Toast – You will be able to toast a total of 9 slices of bread at one go with this toaster oven, and it provides you three types of toasting options.

2. Dual Cook – Experiment with your dishes with this fantastic cooking function, which allows you to combine two different functions, such as baking and roasting, or broiling and baking, and so on.

3. Pizza – Who doesn't like pizza? This oven has a fresh pizza baking option that automatically preheats before baking.

4. Broil – For steak lovers, it is essential that the meat is properly broiled to ensure a juicy and tender texture, and this toaster oven's broil feature will surely ensure it.

5. Bagel – Elevate your breakfast with the addition of a bagel; this option will ensure a soft and properly baked bagel.

6. Waffle – The waffle function is highly reliable for those individuals who are running out of time and need a quick snack to fill your stomach.

7. Bake – The baking option will allow you to bake at your preferred temperature and heating settings with ease.

8. Sandwich – Spread over some cheese along with a few slices of pepperoni on your bread, put it in the oven, press the sandwich option, and, within minutes, your cheese sandwich will be prepared.

9. Convection – This is one function that helps upgrade the other cooking options since it provides uniform airflow in the enclosed space.

10. Keep Warm – At the end of a long day at the office, it's natural for you not to have sufficient energy to prepare food. The keep-warm feature will allow you to heat your food in no time.

11. Leftover – This option will help you revive leftover food in your refrigerator, enabling it to be served fresh.

12. Roast – Glaze your chicken with the incredible roast function of this oven; it will make sure that the food is cooked thoroughly.

13. Speed Convection – For a rapid cooking or baking experience, the speed convection will play an important role in uniform heat distribution.

14. Convection Baking – The convection baking function makes the hassle of baking much easier and faster.

15. Convection Broiling – Broiling takes a fair bit of time in other toaster ovens but this convection broiling system ensures better broiling at a shorter time.

Basic Tips to Get Started

Using any electric appliance requires a lot of safety measures. When the oven is not in use, make sure to turn off the power supply and keep that region dry and clean. You need to go through the entire manual and the provided instructions carefully before operating the toaster oven. Nowadays, children tend to be curious about electronics, so make sure that they use it under adult supervision.

A few of the basic factors to consider while getting started with a toaster oven is the food you're craving. If you have the recipe and the overall preparation procedure, the rest depends on your mixing and adding ingredients in proper portions. We might have made it sound a bit too easy, but when you actually get the hang of using the settings and functions properly, it will totally be that easy.

The best part is, the 15 automated cooking functions will give you freedom when you want to customize your dishes. Besides that, make sure to use your oven regularly. This will keep you practicing and will also make sure that your oven isn't getting rusty.

Tips and Tricks of Usage, Cleaning, and Maintenance

We will be discussing in detail some of the recipes which you can easily cook or bake using Cuisinart Convection Toaster Oven. However, there are some tips and tricks you can incorporate within the process to make it easier. You will be surprised to know how swiftly you can bake cookies and cakes in a toaster oven using the speed convection function.

The durability of a toaster oven depends on its construction and the way you maintain it. Cleaning and maintaining regularly is essential to avoid any technical malfunction. Whenever you're cleaning the toaster, make sure it isn't connected to the power supply. And for that, it is recommended that you use a cleaning agent with the help of a cloth or a sponge.

The additional accessories that are provided with the Cuisinart Convection Toaster Oven such as grill, tray, broiling pan, etc. should be washed separately after every cooking session.

Chapter 2: Breakfast and Brunch

Bacon, Egg and Cheese Breakfast Hash

There is no better option for breakfast!

Prep time and cooking time: 35 minutes | Serves: 4

Ingredients to Use:

- 2 slices of bacon
- 4 tiny potatoes
- 1/4 tomato
- 1 egg
- 1/4 cup of shredded cheese

Step-by-step direction to cook:

1. Preheat the Cuisinart Convection Toaster Oven to 200^{0}C or 400^{0}F on bake mode. Set bits of bacon on a double-layer tin foil.
2. Cut the vegetables to put over the bacon. Crack an egg over it.
3. Shape the tin foil into a bowl and cook it in the oven at 177^{0}C or 350^{0}F for 15-20 minutes. Put some shredded cheese on top.

Nutritional Value per Serving:

Calories: 150.5 kcal, Carbs: 18g, Protein: 6g, Fat: 6g.

Southwestern Hash with Eggs

You don't have to take hours to make a hearty breakfast.

Prep time and cooking time: 70 minutes | Serves: 4

Ingredients To Use:

- 1-1/2 lbs. pork steak
- 1 tsp. vegetable oil
- 1 large potato, peeled and cubed
- 1 medium-sized onion, chopped
- 1 garlic clove, minced
- 1/2 cup green pepper, chopped
- 1 can diced tomatoes and green chilies
- 1 beef bouillon cube
- 1/2 tsp. ground cumin
- 1/2 tsp. salt
- 1/4 tsp. pepper
- 1/8 tsp. cayenne pepper
- 4 eggs
- 3/4 cup shredded cheddar cheese
- 4 corn tortillas (six inches)

Step-by-Step Directions to cook:

1. Cook pork in oil until brown and add potato, onion, garlic, green pepper. Cook for 4 minutes.
2. Stir in tomatoes, bouillon, cumin, salt, pepper, and cayenne. Cook with low heat until potatoes become tender.
3. Create four wells inside the hash and crack eggs into them.
4. Bake it in the Cuisinart Convection Toaster Oven uncovered for 10-12 minutes at 177⁰C or 350⁰F and scatter some cheese over it.
5. Serve over tortillas.

Nutritional Value per Serving:

Calories: 520kcal, Carbs: 29g, Protein: 49g, Fat: 23g.

Maple-Glazed Sausages and Figs

You can get both sweet and savory flavors from this breakfast dish.

Prep time and cooking time: 40 minutes | Serves: 2

Ingredients To Use:

- 2 tbsp. maple syrup
- 2 tbsp. balsamic vinegar
- 2 packages of (12 ounces each) fully cooked chicken, cooked garlic sausages
- 8 fully ripe fresh figs, cut lengthwise
- 1/2 large sweet onion, minced
- 1-1/2 lbs. Swiss chard, with sliced stems, minced leaves
- 2 tsp. olive oil
- Salt and pepper

Step-by-Step Directions to cook:

1. Preheat the Cuisinart Convection Toaster Oven to 232^0C or 450^0F, mix syrup with 1 tbsp. vinegar in a tiny bowl. Put sausages with figs on a one-layer foil-lined oven tray.
2. Roast for 8-10 minutes by grazing the syrup mix throughout the cooking.
3. Cook the onions in the oven in a bowl with plastic wrap for 9 minutes.
4. Mix oil and seasoning with 1 tsp. vinegar. Serve the chards with figs and sausages.

Nutritional Value per Serving:

Calories: 450kcal, Carbs: 42g, Protein: 34g, Fat: 17g.

Asparagus and Leek Quiche with Gruyere

This is a fantastic option for a Sunday brunch.

Prep time and cooking time: 65 minutes | Serves: 4

Ingredients To Use:

- 9-inch tart shell
- 1/2 tbsp. unsalted butter
- 1/2 lb. asparagus, minced into 1/2-inch pieces
- 1 little leek, around 2-3 ounces, with white and light green parts
- Kosher salt and fresh ground black pepper
- 1/4 fresh thyme leaves
- 1/2 cup whole milk and 1/2 cup heavy cream
- 4 big eggs
- 1/2 cup minced Gruyère

Step-by-Step Directions to cook:

1. Whisk milk and heavy cream with eggs in a medium mixing bowl.
2. Put asparagus and leek evenly in the shell. Glug the cream mixture on top and sprinkle minced cheese evenly over it.
3. Preheat the Cuisinart Convection Toaster Oven at 177⁰C or 350⁰F for 25 minutes before placing the quiche inside.
4. After the custard sets completely, broil for 3-5 minutes to make it brown.

Nutritional Value per Serving:

Calories: 194kcal, Carbs: 9g, Protein: 5g, Fat: 15g.

Holiday Brunch Casserole (Grits Casserole)

This grits casserole is fun to make and tastes really good.

Prep time and cooking time: 60 minutes | Serves: 4

Ingredients To Use:

- 4 cups of water
- 1 cup grits
- 1/2 tablespoon salt & paprika
- 1 lb. sausage
- 1/2 cup margarine
- 1/4 lbs. garlic cheese (put 1 tablespoon garlic on white cheese)
- 1/2 cup milk
- 3 eggs

Step-by-Step Directions to cook:

1. Preheat the Cuisinart Convection Toaster Oven at 190°C or 375°F.
2. Fry and drain the sausage. Cook the grits in boiling salted water for 5 minutes.
3. Stir margarine and cheese until it melts before adding milk, eggs, and sausages, and mixing them properly. Pour it inside an 11 -3/4 x 9-3/8 x 1-1/2 " aluminum pan.
4. Bake the mixture at 177°C or 350°F for 30-45 minutes.
5. Spread paprika over the casserole and cover it with foil.

Nutritional Value per Serving:

Calories: 403.2kcal, Carbs: 16.8g, Protein: 16.5g.

Watching Over the Bay Sunday Brunch Benedict

This is a very simple brunch recipe to make.

Prep time and cooking time: 20 minutes | Serves: 4

Ingredients To Use:

- 4 Bays English Muffins cut and toasted
- 4 eggs
- 1 lb. Pancetta, chopped
- Smoky Paprika
- Fresh Cilantro
- Hollandaise sauce
- Pepper

Step-by-Step Directions to cook:

1. Put a muffin in the Cuisinart Convection Toaster Oven on both sides of the plates.
2. Make crisp pancetta in a small pan, cook eggs over easy, and prepare hollandaise sauce on the side.
3. Put pancetta evenly on top of muffins, and eggs over easy above the pancetta.
4. Put hollandaise sauce on top and sprinkle smoky paprika and freshly minced Cilantro.

Nutritional Value per Serving:

Calories: 560kcal, Carbs: 39g, Protein: 43g, Fat: 29g.

Easy Oven Frittata

Try this Frittata recipe by yourself.

Prep time and cooking time: 50 minutes | Serves: 6

Ingredients To Use:

- 8 eggs
- 1 onion; minced
- 1 clove garlic; diced
- 1 cup vegetables
- 1 cup sausage or bacon; minced
- 1 cup cheese; shredded & 1 tsp. Parmesan cheese
- 1 cup milk
- 1 tbsp. flour
- Butter
- Salt and Pepper

Step-by-Step Directions to cook:

1. Preheat the Cuisinart Convection Toaster Oven to 232^0C or 450^0F. Saute onions in a pan to soften them.
2. Cook garlic and any vegetables with meat.
3. Whisk the eggs with milk, flour, and cheese. Put them inside a buttered pan, cook for twenty minutes. Sprinkle salt and pepper on top.

Nutritional Value per Serving:

Calories: 129kcal, Carbs: 2.8g, Fat: 9.6g.

Roasted Brussels Sprouts

Who said brussels sprouts have to be complicated to cook?

Prep time and cooking time: 50 minutes | Serves: 4

Ingredients To Use:

- 2 lbs. Brussels Sprouts, cut
- 1/4 cup olive oil
- Fresh lemon juice
- 1 tsp. minced fresh sage
- 2 tbsp. mixed seasonal Herbs
- Salt and Pepper
- 1/4 cup Pine nuts
- 1/4 cup freshly minced Parmesan-Reggiano

Step-by-Step Directions to cook:

1. Preheat the Cuisinart Convection Toaster Oven to 204⁰C or 400⁰F.
2. Coat the brussels sprouts with all the ingredients evenly in a plastic bag.
3. Put the brussels sprouts inside a huge sheet pan.
4. Roast for 10 minutes inside the oven. Put cheese, pine nuts, and some lemon juice afterward.

Nutritional Value per Serving:

Calories: 135kcal, Carbs: 11g, Protein: 3.9g, Fat: 9.8g.

Cowboy Quiche

This smoky deep-dish meal is all you need in the morning.

Prep time and cooking time: 1 hour 30 minutes | Serves: 8

Ingredients To Use:

- 1 red potato with sliced skin (keep it short)
- 1 onion, minced
- 1/2 jalapeno with minced seeds
- 1 stick butter, melted
- 1 tsp. salt
- Black pepper
- 10 white mushrooms, minced
- 5-7 bacon strips
- 1/2 cup sliced ham
- 1/2 red pepper, minced
- 1/2 green pepper, minced
- 1/4 cup grated Cheddar
- 1/4 cup grated Gruyere
- 6 eggs
- 12 ounces milk
- pint heavy cream
- 1 tsp. ground nutmeg
- 2 unbaked (9-inch) pie doughs

Step-by-Step Directions to cook:

1. Preheat the Cuisinart Convection Toaster Oven to 177^{0}C or 350^{0}F. Put the veggies on a parchment paper-filled tray.
2. Put some melted butter with salt and pepper over vegetables, and bake for 15 minutes.

3. Put mushrooms separately in a parchment paper-filled tray with melted butter on top. Cook for 5 minutes.
4. Cook bacon strips on a different tray until crisp.
5. Put minced ham inside the oven and cook everything properly.
6. Mix all the ingredients to blend properly.
7. Stir eggs, milk, and heavy cream separately, add some salt and black pepper with nutmeg and mix properly.
8. Add the ingredients in a pan containing raw crust with the egg mixture. Bake for 35 minutes.

Nutrition Value per Serving:

Calories: 257.9kcal, Carbs: 24g, Protein: 11.6g, Fat: 9g

Scrambled Eggs

Check out how you can make Scrambled Eggs in a Toaster oven!

Prep time and cooking time: 5 minutes. | Serves: 2

Ingredients To Use:

- 1/2 tbsp. unsalted butter
- 2 big eggs
- 1 tbsp. water kosher salt
- Fresh ground pepper

Step-by-Step Directions to cook:

1. Preheat the Cuisinart Convection Toaster Oven to 149°C or 300°F. Turn the fan on for air circulation.
2. Put seasoned eggs on the lightly greased pan and cover with foil.
3. Cook for 5-10 minutes or until the eggs are set
4. Use a spatula to stir the eggs, and scrape the sides.

Nutritional Value per Serving:

Calories: 149kcal, Carbs: 1g, Protein: 12g, Fat: 6.7g.

Chapter 3: Red Meat Recipes

Salt-and-Pepper Beef Roast

This meat meal will taste the most tender when it is thinly sliced.

Prep time and cooking time: 4.5 hours | Serves: 12-14

Ingredients to Use:

- 4-6lbs boned beef cross rib roast
- 1/4 cup coarse salt
- 1/4 cup sugar
- 2 tbsp. coarse-ground pepper
- 1/2 cup prepared horseradish

Step-by-Step Directions to cook:

1. Mix salt with sugar in a bowl. Pat the mixture on the beef, and marinate for 3-4 hours.
2. Mix 1.5 tsp. salt, pepper, and horseradish.
3. Put the beef on a rack in a 9"x13" pan and rub the horseradish mixture.
4. Roast in 176^0C or 350^0F in the Cuisinart Convection Toaster Oven. Check if the internal temperature is 120-125^{0}C.
5. Rest for 20 minutes, and then slice the meat thinly across the grain.

Nutritional Value per Serving:

Calories: 267kcal, Carbs: 1.3g, Protein: 20g, Fat: 19g.

Prime Rib Roast

This Prime Rib Roast is a show-stealer.

Prep time and cooking time: 1 hr 45 mins | Serves: 4-6

Ingredients to Use:

- Prime Rib Roast
- Butter
- Salt and pepper

Step-by-Step Directions to cook:

1. Cut the fat parts from each side of the meat, and put it inside the Cuisinart Convection Toaster Oven.
2. Cook at 230^0C or 450^0F for 15 minutes. Lower it to 165^0C or 325 afterward.
3. Check if the internal temperature has reached 110^0C or 225^0F and serve.

Nutritional Value per Serving:

Calories: 290kcal, Protein: 19.2g, Fat: 23.1g.

Beef Tenderloin

This is the best dish for any special occasion.

Prep time and cooking time: 1 hour 10 minutes | Serves: 6

Ingredients to Use:

- 5 lbs. Beef Tenderloin
- Vegetable Oil
- Spices, salt, and pepper

Step-by-Step Directions to Cook:

1. Preheat the Cuisinart Convection Toaster Oven to 180^0C or 350^0F. Cut extra fat from it.
2. Gently rub tenderloin with vegetable oil and seasoning.
3. Cook it in the oven for 20-30 mins.

Nutritional Value per Serving:

Calories: 179kcal, Protein: 26g, Fat: 7.6g.

Perfect Rump Roast

Rump roast makes for a wonderful Sunday dinner meal.

Prep time and cooking time: 2 hours | Serves: 5

Ingredients to Use:

- 4lb rump roast
- 3 Garlic cloves
- 1 tbsp. each of salt, pepper
- 1 onion
- 1 cup water

Step-by-Step Directions to Cook:

1. Preheat the Cuisinart Convection Toaster Oven to 260^{0}C or 500^{0}F
2. Make 4-5 cuts on the roast, and fill with salt, pepper, and garlic.
3. Season some more before searing for 20 mins. Add water and minced onion.
4. Cook in the oven at 180^{0}C or 350^{0}F for 1.5 hours.

Nutritional Value per Serving:

Calories: 916.8kcal, Carbs: 4.4g, Protein: 94.6g, Fat: 55.2g.

Rosemary Roasted Leg of Lamb

Leg of lamb is the star of Easter celebrations.

Prep time and cooking time: 70 minutes | Serves: 6-8

Ingredients to Use:

- 5-6lbs boneless leg of lamb
- 2 tbsp. olive oil
- 5-6 cloves garlic, peeled and minced
- 2 tbsp. minced rosemary leaves
- 1 tbsp. kosher salt
- Freshly ground black pepper

Step-by-Step Directions to cook:

1. Preheat the Cuisinart Convection Toaster Oven to 190°C or 375°F. Graze the lamb with olive oil.
2. Pat all the ingredients on the lamb and put it in the baking pan.
3. Cook for 90 mins and check if the internal temperature has reached 125°C or 250°F for rare and 135°C or 275°F for medium-rare.
4. Remove it from the oven, and wrap with aluminum foil.

Nutritional Value per Serving:

Calories: 136kcal, Carbs: 0.3g, Protein: 23g, Fat: 1.4g.

Slow Roasted Beef Short Ribs

Beef short ribs always taste delicious with this recipe.

Prep time and cooking time: 3 hours 10 minutes | Serves: 6

Ingredients to Use:

- 5lbs beef short ribs
- 1/3 cup brown sugar
- 1 tsp. garlic powder
- 1 tsp. onion powder
- 1/4 tsp. marjoram
- 1/2 tsp. kosher salt
- 1/4 tsp. thyme
- 1 pinch cayenne pepper

Step-by-Step Directions to cook:

1. Pat the ribs dry.
2. Rub the ingredients on each rib, put them in a sealed plastic bag, and freeze overnight.
3. Preheat the Cuisinart Convection Toaster Oven to 150°C or 300°F, and put ribs on a rack in a roasting pan.
4. Roast for around 3 hours.

Nutritional Value per Serving:

Calories: 791kcal, Carbs: 19g, Protein: 79g, Fat: 42g.

Sirloin Roast Beef

This succulent beef dish can be perfect for Christmas.

Prep time and cooking time: 1 hour 45 minutes | Serves: 6

Ingredients to Use:

- 3.3 lbs. Sirloin of Beef
- 2 tbsp. vegetable oil
- 6 ounces red wine
- 14 ounces beef consomme

Step-by-Step Directions to cook:

1. Preheat the Cuisinart Convection Toaster Oven to 200^0C or 400^0F.
2. Season the sirloin and cook it at medium heat in oil for 5 mins, turning regularly.
3. Roast it in the oven for 15 mins to make it medium-rare. Flip it halfway.
4. Remove it when the internal temperature is 145^0F, and cover with foil.
5. Make a gravy with the fat residue on the pan and some wine.
6. Add beef consomme to the sauce and simmer for 5 mins. Strain when completed and pour on the roast.

Nutritional Value per Serving:

Calories: 179kcal, Protein: 22g, Fat: 9.4g.

Oven Roasted Hamburgers

These juicy hamburgers can be made at any time of the year!

Prep time and cooking time: 25 minutes | Serves: 6

Ingredients to Use:

- 1-1/2 tsp. kosher salt
- 2 lbs. ground beef
- 1 tbsp. Worcestershire sauce
- 1/2 tsp. freshly ground black pepper
- 6 toasted hamburger buns
- Hamburger toppings

Step-by-Step Directions to cook:

1. Preheat the Cuisinart Convection Toaster Oven to 230^0C or 450^0F, and line a rimmed baking sheet with aluminum foil with some salt to absorb drippings.
2. Season 1-2 inch lumps of meat by hand and split up meat into 6 parts to shape into 3"x1" disks
3. Place burgers an inch apart on a wire rack and roast for 10-16 mins at 135^0C or 250^0F for medium-rare meat.

Nutritional Value per Serving:

Calories: 131.6kcal, Carbs: 8.7g, Protein: 13.1g, Fat: 4.1g.

Pan-Seared Oven Roasted Strip Steak

This is a quick-and-easy dish that you can even serve in restaurants.

Prep time and cooking time: 30 minutes | Serves: 2

Ingredients to Use:

- One 3-inch Strip Steak
- 1 tbsp. Butter
- Meat Tenderizer
- Coarsely Ground Black Pepper

Step-by-Step Directions to cook:

1. Cut and season the room-temperature meat.
2. Preheat the Cuisinart Convection Toaster Oven to 200⁰C or 400⁰F.
3. Sear steak in butter over medium-high heat evenly for 2-3 mins after an hour of resting.
4. Cook in the oven for 7 mins to achieve medium-rare.

Nutritional Value per Serving:

Calories: 253.6kcal, Carbs: 0.2g, Protein: 21.1g, Fat: 18.1g, .

London Broil Steak

A perfectly tender and flavorful meat dish.

Prep time and cooking time: 75 minutes | Serves: 6

Ingredients to Use:

- 2 lb. London broil top-round steak
- Kosher salt
- Freshly ground black pepper
- 1/4 cup extra-virgin olive oil
- 1/2 Lemon juice
- 2 tbsp. brown sugar
- 1 tbsp. Worcestershire sauce
- 4 cloves garlic, diced
- 1/4 cup Balsamic vinegar

Step-by-Step Directions to cook:

1. Marinate the steak in the refrigerator for at least 20 mins.
2. Preheat the Cuisinart Convection Toaster Oven to 190°C or 375°F, and cook the steak for 6-8 mins on each side.

Nutritional Value per Serving:

Calories: 173kcal, Protein: 26.1g, Fat: 7.7g.

Chapter 4: Poultry Recipes

Chicken Thighs with Rosemary

Roasted chicken thigh with rosemary springs and some vegetables is perfect for a great brunch.

Prep time and cooking time: 40 minutes | Serves: 4

Ingredients to use

- 4 chicken thighs, with the bone and skin
- Rosemary sprigs
- A large potato, cut into cubes
- 1 onion
- 2 tbsp. of olive oil
- 2 garlic cloves
- Salt and pepper
- 1/2 tsp. of chicken seasoning powder

Step-by-Step Directions to cook it:

1. Preheat the Cuisinart Convection Toaster Oven at 218^{0}C or 425^{0}F.
2. Put the rosemary sprigs on the baking pan with cooking spray.
3. Bake the remaining ingredients for half an hour.
4. Season the chicken thighs and bake for 35 minutes.

Nutritional value per serving:

Calories: 670 kcal, Carbs: 14g, Protein: 47g, Fat: 46g.

Baked Chicken Tenders

Who doesn't love chicken tenders? They are one of the most popular snacks you could have.

Prep time and cooking time: 45 minutes | Serves: 6-8

Ingredients to Use:

- 1-1/2 lb. of boneless chicken tenders
- 2 eggs
- 2 tsp. of butter, melted
- 2/3 cup of graham crackers
- 2/3 cup of breadcrumbs
- Barbecue sauce
- Salt and pepper for seasoning

Step-by-Step Directions to cook it:

1. Preheat the Cuisinart Convection Toaster Oven to 232^{0}C or 450^{0}F and spray some oil on the baking pan
2. Combine the crackers, breadcrumbs, and butter until smooth.
3. Beat the eggs in another bowl with salt and pepper.
4. Dip the chicken pieces in the eggs first and then the breadcrumbs.
5. Bake for 15-18 minutes.

Nutritional value per serving:

Calories: 362kcal, Carbs: 16.5g, Protein: 58g, Fat: 5.8g,

Chicken Curry Salad

You can even take the healthy route with a toaster oven. Go on and make a chicken salad.

Prep time and cooking time: 55 minutes | Serves: 4

Ingredients to Use:

- 3 chicken breasts cut into cubes
- 1 tbsp. Dijon mustard
- 1/2 cup of mayo
- Chopped celery
- A cup of red grapes, cut into halves
- 1 tbsp. sour cream
- Salt and pepper for seasoning
- 2 tbsp. cilantro, chopped
- 1-1/2 tbsp. of spice mix

Step-by-Step Directions to cook it:

1. Cook boneless chicken for half an hour at 149^0C or 300^0F in the Cuisinart Convection Toaster Oven.
2. Combine the remaining ingredients.
3. Add the cooked chicken and grapes to the mixture. Mix them well.
4. Put a plastic wrap on the bowl and refrigerate overnight before serving.

Nutritional value per serving:

Calories: 325kcal, Carbs: 13g, Protein: 37g, Fat: 14g.

Herb Roasted Turkey Breast

Moving away from the chicken recipes to another delicacy.

Prep time and cooking time: 2 hours and 40 minutes | Serves: 6

Ingredients to Use:

- 1/2 tsp. of minced garlic
- One turkey breast, thawed
- 1 tsp. thyme, ground
- 1/2 cup of softened butter
- Crushed rosemary leaves
- Salt and pepper for seasoning

Step-by-Step Directions to cook it:

1. Preheat the Cuisinart Convection Toaster Oven at 204°C or 400°F.
2. Place the turkey breast on the pan after spraying cooking spray.
3. Mix the remaining ingredients and use a brush to rub it onto the breast evenly.
4. Roast for 2-1/2 hours and rest for 15 minutes after taking it out.

Nutritional value per serving:

Calories: 360kcal, Carbs: 1g, Protein: 72g, Fat: 5g.

Shredded Chicken Sandwich

A sandwich is a great snack for almost any time of the day.

Prep time and cooking time: 25 minutes | Serves: 2

Ingredients to use;

- Shredded chicken
- Mayo
- Lettuce
- Salt and pepper
- 2 slices of whole-grain bread

Step-by-Step Directions to cook it:

1. Toast bread with butter in the Cuisinart Convection Toaster Oven.
2. Mix up all the other ingredients until smooth.
3. Cut the slices into halves and fill it up with the mixture.

Nutritional value per serving:

Calories: 368kcal, Carbs: 51g, Protein: 25g, Fat: 7.2g.

Dijon Stuffed Chicken

This is another great dish you could try out for brunch.

Prep time and cooking time: 45 minutes | Serves: 4

Ingredients to Use:

- 2 chicken breasts
- 1 potato, cubed
- Dijon mustard1 tsp.
- Salt and pepper
- 2 slices of provolone cheese
- 2 tsp. of olive oil
- Half an Apple
- Spinach

Step-by-Step Directions to cook it:

1. Preheat the Cuisinart Convection Toaster Oven to 218^{0}C or 425^{0}F.
2. Bake the potatoes for 10 minutes.
3. Make 2 slits on the breasts and rub in some dijon mustard.
4. Put the apple slices and cheese slices in the slits and rub with salt, pepper, and olive oil.
5. Bake for 30 minutes.

Nutritional value per serving:

Calories: 340kcal, Carbs: 6g, Protein: 35g, Fat: 19g.

Apple Herb Roasted Turkey

Here's another turkey dish anyone would love to try out.

Prep time and cooking time: 4 hours and 45 minutes | Serves: 16

Ingredients to Use:

- 1 whole turkey
- 4 apples, sliced
- Half a teaspoon of paprika
- 1/2 tsp. garlic powder
- 1/2 tsp. black pepper
- 2 sweet onions, quartered
- Butter

Step-by-Step Directions to cook it:

1. Make the herbed butter in advance and refrigerate.
2. Preheat the Cuisinart Convection Toaster Oven to 163^{0}C or 325^{0}F.
3. Cut off the turkey neck and loosen the membranes under the skin.
4. Put herbed butter and apples inside the skin.
5. Use the rest of the apples and onions as the stuffing.
6. Make the spice mixture and rub it on.
7. Bake for 3-4 hours at 74^{0}C or 165^{0}F.

Nutritional value per serving:

Calories: 626kcal, Carbs: 10g, Protein: 72g, Fat: 31g.

Breakfast Strata

If you love eggs at breakfast, you will love this Strata that serves 24 people.

Prep time and cooking time: 8 hours | Serves: 8

Ingredients to Use:

- 18 eggs
- 2 packs of croutons
- 1 pack of cheddar
- Salt & pepper
- 1 pack of chopped spinach
- 3 cups of milk
- 3 cups chopped ham
- 1 jar Red Peppers

Step-by-Step Directions to cook it:

1. Preheat the Cuisinart Convection Toaster Oven to 135^{0}C or 275^{0}F.
2. Spray the pan with a non-stick spray.
3. Spread layers of ham, spinach, cheese, and croutons, and red peppers.
4. Pour eggs mixed with milk and seasoning in the pan and refrigerate.
5. Bake for 2 hours and leave to rest for 15 minutes.

Nutritional value per serving:

Calories: 140kcal, Carbs: 6g, Protein: 16g, Fat: 5g.

Scrambled Eggs Wonton Cups

Here's one with bite-sized wonton goodness. Try it out!

Prep time and cooking time: 25 minutes | Serves: 3

Ingredients to Use:

- 6 wonton wrappers
- 6 eggs
- 3 Breakfast sausages
- 2 large peppers
- 4 mushrooms
- 3 onions
- Butter
- Salt and pepper to taste

Step-by-Step Directions to cook it:

1. Preheat the Cuisinart Convection Toaster Oven to 177⁰C or 350⁰F.
2. Make the scrambled eggs.
3. Fold the wrappers brushed with butter into the muffin pan
4. Mix the ingredients in a bowl and put it in the wrappers.
5. Bake for 10 minutes.

Nutritional value per serving:

Calories: 130kcal, Carbs: 7g, Protein: 9g, Fat: 7g.

Sheet Pan Shakshuka

Try out this unique egg dish with some toasted bread!

Prep time and cooking time: 25 minutes | Serves: 4

Ingredients to Use:

- 4 large eggs
- 1 large Anaheim chili, chopped
- 2 tbsp. vegetable oil
- 1/2 cup onion, chopped
- 1 tsp. cumin, ground
- 2 minced garlic cloves
- 1/2 cup feta cheese
- 1/2 tsp. paprika
- 1 can of tomatoes
- Salt & pepper

Step-by-Step Directions to cook it:

1. Saute the chili and onions in vegetable oil until tender.
2. Pour in the remaining ingredients except for eggs and cook until thick.
3. Make 4 pockets to pour in the eggs.
4. Bake for 10 minutes at 191^{0}C or 375^{0}F in the Cuisinart Convection Toaster Oven.
5. Top it off with feta.

Nutritional value per serving:

Calories: 219kcal, Carbs: 20g, Protein: 10g, Fat: 11g.

Chapter 5: Seafood Recipes

Sheet Pan Shrimp Fajitas

Who doesn't love shrimp fajitas? Try out this quick recipe today.

Prep Time and Cooking Time: 20 minutes | Serves: 2

Ingredients to Use:

- 8 oz. shrimp, deveined and peeled
- 1 minced garlic clove
- 2 tbsp. lime juice
- 1 tbsp. olive oil
- Chili pepper & cayenne pepper
- Sour cream
- 2 avocados, sliced
- Cilantro, chopped
- 4 tortillas
- Salt and pepper

Step-by-Step Directions to cook it:

1. Mix all the spices and seasonings and add it to the shrimps.
2. Preheat the Cuisinart Convection Toaster Oven at 177^{0}C or 350^{0}F.
3. Bake the shrimps in the pan with chili peppers
4. Serve in tortillas

Nutritional value per serving:

Calories: 408kcal, Carbs: 76g, Protein: 42g, Fat: 6g.

Broiled Chipotle Tilapia

Try out this amazing seafood chipotle with delicious Tilapia.

Prep Time and Cooking Time: 20 minutes | Serves: 2

Ingredients to use:

- 1/2 lbs. tilapia fillets
- 1 tsp. lime juice
- Cilantro, chopped
- 3 tsp. chipotle
- 1 avocado, peeled and halved
- 3 tbsp. sour cream
- Mayo, 1 tbsp.

Step-by-Step Directions to cook it:

1. Blend the ingredients except for the fish.
2. Brush the fish fillets with the mix.
3. Broil the fish at 132^{0}C or 270^{0}F in the Cuisinart Convection Toaster Oven for 10 minutes.

Nutritional value per serving:

Calories: 385kcal, Carbs: 65g, Protein: 18g, Fat: 7g,

Broiled Crab Cakes With Herb Sauce

This crab cake makes for a perfect afternoon snack.

Prep Time and Cooking Time: 25 minutes | Serves: 4

Ingredients to use:

- 1 lb. crab meat
- 1 large egg
- 1 minced garlic clove
- 1/4 parsley, chopped
- 1 tsp. seafood seasoning
- Salt & pepper
- 1 shallot
- 1 tbsp. brown mustard
- 4 tbsp. mayo
- 1 tbsp. flour

Step-by-Step Directions to cook it:

1. Mix mayo, eggs, mustard, seasoning, and flour until smooth
2. Stir in the lump of crab meat along with shallots, parsley, garlic.
3. Make 4 balls and place them on the pan
4. Broil in the Cuisinart Convection Toaster Oven at 121C or 250⁰F for 8 minutes.

Nutritional value per serving:

Calories: 240kcal, Carbs: 8g, Protein: 16g, Fat: 16g.

Dijon Salmon with Green Beans

Check out one of the best salmon dish recipes.

Prep Time and Cooking Time: 30 minutes | Serves: 2-3

Ingredients to use

- 1 tbsp. dijon mustard
- 3/4 lbs. salmon fillets
- 1 tbsp. soy sauce
- 2 garlic cloves
- 1/2 small red bell pepper, sliced
- Salt and pepper
- 2 tbsp. olive oil
- 6 oz. green beans, trimmed
- 1 small leek, sliced

Step-by-Step Directions to cook it:

1. Preheat the Cuisinart Convection Toaster Oven to 204°C or 400°F.
2. Mix soy sauce, olive oil, garlic, and mustard.
3. Mix the remaining ingredients with olive oil.
4. Place the salmon fillets, brushed with the oil mix, on the pan with the veggies around
5. Bake for 15 minutes.

Nutritional value per serving:

Calories: 295kcal, Carbs: 5g, Protein: 23g, Fat: 20g.

Baked Coconut Shrimp

Another shrimp recipe for your exquisite taste buds!

Prep Time and Cooking Time: 20 minutes | Serves: 8-10

Ingredients to use:

- 1 lb. large shrimp, deveined
- 1 cup chutney
- 1/2 tsp. ground curry
- 2 tbsp. sliced green onion
- 1 tsp. salt and pepper
- 1 cup breadcrumbs
- Cilantro, chopped
- 1/2 tsp. red peppers, crushed
- 3/4 cup coconut, shredded
- 1 egg

Step-by-Step Directions to cook it:

1. Mix the green onion, chutney, curry, onion, and red pepper
2. Preheat the Cuisinart Convection Toaster Oven to 232^{0}C or 450^{0}F.
3. Mix the flour with salt, coconut, and breadcrumbs.
4. Whisk the egg white.
5. Dip the shrimp in the egg and then in the crumb mix.
6. Arrange them on the pan and bake for 10 minutes.

Nutritional value per serving:

Calories: 167kcal, Carbs: 14g, Protein: 14g, Fat: 6g.

Fish and Chips

Here's some plain old fish and chips, the classic snack.

Prep Time and Cooking Time: 1 hour | Serves: 4

- 4 pieces of cod, 6 oz. each
- 8 thyme sprigs
- 1-3/4 lb. potato, cubed
- 1 lemon, cut in half
- 2 tbsp. capers
- Salt & pepper
- 1 garlic clove
- 4 tbsp. olive oil

Step-by-Step Directions to cook it:

1. Preheat the Cuisinart Convection Toaster Oven to 232^{0}C or 450^{0}F.
2. Bake the potatoes, olive oil, salt, pepper, and 4 thyme sprigs for 30 minutes.
3. Brush the cod with lemon and put the remaining ingredients on top of the cod
4. Drizzle some olive oil and bake for another 12 minutes.

Nutritional value per serving:

Calories: 378kcal, Carbs: 33g, Protein: 34g, Fat: 12g.

Pesto Salmon

Add a little twist to baked salmon with pesto.

Prep Time and Cooking Time: 35 minutes | Serves: 4

Ingredients to use:

- 4 salmon fillets, 1-1/4 lb. each
- 2 tbsp. thawed pesto
- 2 tbsp. white wine vinegar
- 1 lemon, cut into halves
- 2 tbsp. Toasted pine nuts

Step-by-Step Directions to cook it:

1. Place the salmon fillets on the pan after spraying cooking spray
2. Preheat the Cuisinart Convection Toaster Oven to 232°C or 450°F.
3. Marinade the fillets with lemon juice, pesto, and white wine vinegar
4. Broil for 15 minutes.

Nutritional value per serving:

Calories: 326kcal, Carbs: 1.5g, Protein: 39g, Fat: 17g.

Garlic Butter Orange Roughy

This one is considered quite a delicacy in some parts of the world.

Prep Time and Cooking Time: 30 minutes | Serves: 4

Ingredients to use:

- 2 tbsp. butter
- 1/2 lb. orange Roughy, filleted
- 1 tbsp. olive oil
- 3 minced garlic cloves
- Salt & pepper

Step-by-Step Directions to cook it:

1. Preheat the Cuisinart Convection Toaster Oven to 190°C or 375°F.
2. Melt butter in a pan with garlic cloves and olive oil.
3. Season the fillets and pour the garlic butter.
4. Bake for 20 minutes

Nutritional value per serving:

Calories: 255kcal, Carbs: 2g, Protein: 19g, Fat: 19g.

Mustard Crusted Salmon

Here's another variation of the classic salmon fillet.

Prep Time And Cooking Time: 25 minutes | Serves: 4

Ingredients to use:

- 1 tsp. Dijon mustard
- 6 oz. salmon filets
- 1 tsp. chives, chopped
- 1 tbsp. lemon juice
- 2 tbsp. sour cream
- Salt and pepper
- 1 tbsp. breadcrumbs (panko)

Step-by-Step Directions to cook it:

1. Preheat the Cuisinart Convection Toaster Oven at 190°C or 375°F with broil mode.
2. Season the fillets with salt, pepper, and dijon mustard.
3. Sprinkle breadcrumbs on top
4. Bake for 8-9 minutes
5. Serve with sour cream and lemon juice

Nutritional value per serving:

Calories: 350kcal, Carbs: 7g, Protein: 36g, Fat: 19g.

Baked Sole with Asparagus

Ending the seafood chapter with this fantastic baked Sole recipe.

Prep Time and Cooking Time: 25 minutes | Serves: 4

- 2 lbs. asparagus
- 1 tsp. olive oil
- 3 tbsp. parmesan, grated
- Salt and black pepper
- 2 tbsp. panko breadcrumbs
- 1 tsp. minced chives
- 2 tbsp. mayo
- 2 fillets of sole, 8 oz.
- 1/4 lemon, cut into wedges

Step-by-Step Directions to cook it:

1. Preheat the Cuisinart Convection Toaster Oven at 232^0C or 450^0F.
2. Season the asparagus with olive oil and seasoning
3. Mix breadcrumbs, cheese, salt, and pepper.
4. Mix mayo with chives and brush this on to the fillets
5. Press the brushed sides with the cheese mix
6. Bake for 15 minutes. Serve with lemon juice.

Nutritional value per serving:

Calories: 284kcal, Carbs: 18g, Protein: 35g, Fat: 9g.

Chapter 6: Vegetarian recipe

Sweet Potato Toast

The toaster oven makes the potato crispy on the outside and soft and tender on the inside.

Prep Time and Cooking Time: 25 minutes | Serves: 2

Ingredients To Use:

- 1 large sweet potato, cut
- Avocado/guacamole
- Hummus
- Radish/Tomato (optional)
- Salt & Pepper
- Lemon slice

Step-by-Step Directions to cook it:

1. Toast the potatoes in the Cuisinart Convection Toaster Oven for 10 minutes on each side.
2. Spread mashed avocado, add seasoning, top it with radish slices and squeeze a lime over it.
3. Or, spread hummus, seasoning, and your choice of greens.

Nutritional value per serving:

Calories: 114 kcal, Carbs: 13g, Protein: 2g, Fat: 7g.

Stuffed Portabella Mushroom

Make gorgeous stuffed portabella mushrooms today with your toaster oven.

Prep Time and Cooking Time: 35 minutes | Serves: 2

Ingredients To Use:

- 2 large portabella mushrooms
- Breadcrumbs
- Nutritional yeast (gives a cheesy, savory flavor)
- 1 cup tofu ricotta
- 1/2 cup canned marinara sauce
- 1 cup spinach
- 1/2 tsp. garlic powder
- 1 tsp. dry basil & 1 tsp. dry thyme
- Salt & pepper

Step-by-Step Directions to cook it:

1. Make ricotta with tofu, lemon juice, nutritional yeast, salt, and pepper. Mix the tofu ricotta, spinach, thyme, basil, marinara sauce, and seasoning.
2. Brush marinara sauce on each mushroom and stuff the filling. Top it with breadcrumbs, nutritional yeast, and some olive oil.
3. Bake for 15 minutes at 230⁰C or 450⁰F in your Cuisinart Convection Toaster Oven.

Nutritional value per serving:

Calories: 275kcal, Carbs: 10.4g, Protein: 23.0g, Fat: 19.5g.

Pumpkin Quesadillas

Make some amazing quesadillas in a matter of minutes with simple ingredients.

Prep Time and Cooking Time: 15minutes | Serves: 3

Ingredients To Use:

- 1/2 canned pumpkin (pure)
- 2 gluten-free tortillas
- 1/2 cup refried beans
- 1-2 tbsp. nutritional yeast
- 1 tsp. onion powder
- 1 tsp. garlic powder
- Pinch of cayenne
- Salt & pepper

Step-by-Step Directions to cook it:

1. Mix the pumpkin with nutritional yeast, onion powder, garlic powder, cayenne, salt, and pepper.
2. Spread the pumpkin paste mixture in one tortilla and the refried beans in another.
3. Sandwich them together and toast in the Cuisinart Convection Toaster Oven for 5 minutes

Nutritional value per serving:

Calories: 282kcal, Carbs: 37g, Protein: 13g, Fat: 10g.

Toasted-Baked Tofu cubes

Here's simple and easy toasted tofu you can indulge in a matter of minutes.

Prep Time and Cooking Time: 30 minutes | Serves: 2

Ingredients To Use:

- 1/2 block of tofu, cubed
- 1 tbsp. olive oil
- 1 tbsp. nutritional yeast
- 1 tbsp. flour
- 1/4 tsp. black pepper
- 1 tsp. sea salt
- 1/2 tsp. garlic powder

Step-by-Step Directions to cook it:

1. Combine all the ingredients with tofu
2. Preheat the Cuisinart Convection Toaster Oven at 230°C or 400°F.
3. Bake tofu on a lined baking tray for 15-30 minutes, turn it around every 10 minutes.

Nutritional value per serving:

Calories: 100kcal, Carbs: 5g, Protein: 8g, Fat 6g.

Stuffed Squash

You can whip up his delicious stuffed squash easily using your trusty toaster oven.

Prep Time and Cooking Time: 90 minutes | Serves: 4

Ingredients To Use:

- Acorn squash, halved and deseeded
- 2 cups cooked quinoa
- 1/2 edamame (shelled)
- 1/2 corn kernels
- 1/4 cranberries
- Some scallions, basil, and mint (thinly sliced)
- 2 tbsp. Olive oil
- Salt and pepper
- Lemon juice

Step-by-Step Directions to cook it:

1. Brush squash pieces with olive oil, salt, and pepper.
2. Bake it at 176^{0}C or 350^{0}F for 35 minutes in the Cuisinart Convection Toaster Oven.
3. Prepare the filling by mixing all the remaining ingredients. Stuff baked squash with filling and bake for another 15 minutes.

Nutritional value per serving:

Calories: 272kcal, Carbs: 45g, Protein: 7g, Fat 9g.

Eggplant Pizza

A delicious gluten-free pizza to curb your cravings.

Prep Time and Cooking Time: 45 minutes | Serves: 2

Ingredients To Use:

- Eggplant (sliced 1/4 -inch)
- Gluten-free pizza dough
- 1 cup pizza sauce
- Fresh rosemary and basil
- Cheese
- Garlic cloves, chopped
- Red pepper, salt, and pepper
- Olive oil

Step-by-Step Directions to cook it:

1. Rub eggplant slices with olive oil and rosemary, salt and pepper, and bake for 25 mins at 218^0C or 425^0F in the Cuisinart Convection Toaster Oven
2. Roll the dough round and spread the remaining ingredients on top.
3. Preheat the oven at 230^0C or 450^0F at pizza-setting and bake the pizza for 10 minutes.

Nutritional value per serving:

Calories: 260kcal, Carbs: 24g, Protein: 9g, Fat 14g.

Sriracha Roasted Potatoes

Try some spicy roasted potatoes to make your day.

Prep Time and Cooking Time: 40 minutes | Servings: 3

Ingredients To Use:

- 3 potatoes, diced
- 2-3 tsp. sriracha
- 1/4 garlic powder
- Salt & pepper
- Olive oil
- Chopped fresh parsley

Step-by-Step Directions to cook it:

1. Combine the potatoes with the remaining ingredients.
2. Preheat the Cuisinart Convection Toaster Oven at 230°C or 450°F.
3. Line the pan with olive oil and spread the coated potatoes. Sprinkle parsley.
4. Bake for 30 minutes.

Nutritional value per serving:

Calories 147kcal, Carbs: 24.4, Protein: 3g, Fat 4.7g.

Brussel Sprouts, Mango, Avocado Salsa Tacos

Indulge in homemade healthy tacos!

Prep Time and Cooking Time: 40 minutes | Serves: 4

Ingredients to Use:

- 4 taco shells
- 8 ounces brussels sprouts, diced
- Half a mango, diced
- Half of an avocado, diced
- 1/2 cup black beans, cooked
- 2 tbsp. onions, chopped
- 1/4 cup cilantro, chopped
- 1 tbsp. jalapeno, chopped
- Lime juice
- Olive oil
- 1 tbsp. taco seasoning
- Salt & Pepper

Step-by-Step Directions to cook it:

1. Preheat the Cuisinart Convection Toaster Oven at 230⁰C or 400⁰F.
2. Mix the sprouts with taco seasoning, olive oil and salt and pepper on the pan.
3. Roast for 15 mins. Turn every 5 mins.
4. To make the salsa, combine the mango, avocado, black beans, lime juice, cilantro, onion, jalapeno, salt, and pepper.
5. Cook taco shells and fill it with the sprouts and salsa.

Nutritional value per serving:

Calories 407kcal, Carbs: 63.20g, Protein: 11.4g, Fat: 13.9g.

Spaghetti Squash Burrito Bowls

Try these decadent squash bowls to warm up your heart.

Prep Time and Cooking Time: 1 hour | Serves: 2

Ingredients To Use:

- 1 small spaghetti squash
- Zucchini, diced
- 1/4 onion, diced
- Bell peppers, diced
- 3/4 cup black beans, cooked
- 1/2 cup corn kernels
- 1/2 cup salsa
- 2 ounces cheese (optional)
- Olive oil
- 1/2 tsp. dried oregano
- 1/4 tsp. ground cumin
- Salt & pepper

Step-by-Step Directions to cook it:

1. Preheat the Cuisinart Convection Toaster Oven at 230^{0}C or 425^{0}F on bake setting
2. Microwave the squash for 4 minutes and then cut it in half. Scoop out the seeds.
3. Rub oil, salt, and pepper all over the squash and bake it for 45 minutes.
4. Make the filling by stir-frying bell pepper, zucchini, oregano, corn, salt, and pepper for 10 minutes. Add the salsa and black beans.

5. Scrape squash flesh to make spaghetti and toss in the vegetables.
6. Bake them at 176^{0}C or 350^{0}F for 10 minutes and then broil for 1-2 minutes.

Nutritional value per serving:

Calories: 390kcal, Carbs: 51.4g, Protein: 15.7g, Fat 17.1g.

Baked Oatmeal

This wholesome breakfast is perfect to start your day.

Prep Time and Cooking Time: 45 minutes | Serves: 2

Ingredients To Use:

- 1 cup original oats
- 1 banana
- 1/4 cup pecans
- 1/2 cup milk
- 1 tbsp. flax meal
- 2 tsp. olive oil
- 2 tsp. maple syrup
- 1/2 tsp. baking powder
- 1/2 tsp. ground cinnamon & salt
- 1/2 tsp. vanilla-extract

Step-by-Step Directions to cook it:

1. Preheat the Cuisinart Convection Toaster Oven at 176^{0}C or 350^{0}F on the baking setting.
2. Make a batter with mashed banana and all the ingredients.
3. Grease a 7x5-inch dish and pour your batter into it. Bake it for 25-35 minutes.

Nutritional value per serving:

Calories: 235kcal, Carbs: 28.6g, Protein: 4.9g, Fat: 13.2g

Chapter 7: Pizza, Bread, and Sandwich

Toaster Oven Pizza Sandwiches

This quick breakfast meal is a perfect snack for kids.

Prep Time and Cooking Time: 5minutes | Serves: 1

Ingredients to use:

- 1 French bread sandwich roll, sliced
- 5 tsp. pizza sauce
- 15-20 slices pepperoni
- 1 cup mozzarella cheese, shredded

Step-by-Step Directions to cook it:

1. Preheat the Cuisinart Convection Toaster Oven to 250°C or 482°F.
2. Spread pizza sauce on the bread.
3. Add toppings, cheese, and pepperoni on each slice of bread.
4. Toast it until the cheese melts.

Nutritional value per serving:

Calories: 752.1kcal, Carbs: 33.5 g, Protein: 35.2 g, Fat: 15.7g.

Veg Pizza

This recipe includes healthy ingredients and is also easy to prepare.

Prep Time and Cooking Time: 20 minutes | Serves: 2

Ingredients to use:

- 1 cup tomatoes, sliced
- Capsicum, sliced
- 4 baby corns
- 1-2 tsp. pizza sauce
- 1 cup mozzarella cheese
- 3.5 cups all-purpose flour
- 1.5 tsp. oregano seasoning
- Salt
- 1.5 tsp. yeast
- 2-3 tsp. oil
- 1.5 cup of water

Step-by-Step Directions to cook it:

1. Make pizza dough with all-purpose flour adding oil, salt, yeast, and water.
2. Spread the remaining ingredients on the pizza base made of dough.
3. Preheat the Cuisinart Convection Toaster Oven and bake for 10 minutes.

Nutritional value per serving:

Calories: 300kcal, Carbs: 37.5g, Protein: 15g, Fat: 10g.

Toaster Oven-baked Grilled Cheese

This is a crispy, yummy, grilled cheese sandwich that oozes with cheese in every bite.

Prep Time and Cooking Time: 10 minutes | Serves: 1

Ingredients to use:

- 2 slices bread
- 1-2 tsp. mayonnaise
- 2-3 tsp. cheddar cheese
- Fresh spinach

Step-by-Step Directions to cook it:

1. Preheat the Cuisinart Convection Toaster Oven to 200^{0}C or 400^{0}F.
2. Spread mayonnaise and cheese on the bread.
3. Bake for 5-7 minutes. Add the spinach.

Nutritional value per serving:

Calories: 353kcal, Carbs: 42.1g, Protein: 18.9g, Fat: 7.8g.

Cheese Chili Toast

Creamy cheese toast can be a delicious breakfast meal.

Prep Time and Cooking time: 10 minutes | Serves: 2

Ingredients to use:

- 2-4 slices bread
- Capsicum, chopped
- Salt & pepper
- 1-2 Chilies
- 20gm cheese, grated
- 10gm cream
- Oil

Step-by-Step Directions to cook it:

1. Place the bread on the baking pan.
2. Make a mixture of oil, capsicums, peppers, salt, and chilies.
3. Apply the mixture on bread and grated cheese
4. Bake at 180 degrees or 350°F or 177°C for 5-7 minutes in the Cuisinart Convection Toaster Oven. You're all set.

Nutritional value per serving:

Calories: 135cal, Carbs: 11.6g, Protein: 7.1g, Fat: 6.5g.

Hot Ham and Cheese Sandwich

Hot ham sandwiches are a nutritious and quick meal for lunch at home or work.

Prep Time and Cooking time: 13 minutes | Serves: 2

Ingredients to use:

- 2-4 sandwich bread
- Olive oil
- 1/4 tsp. oregano & basil
- 4 ounces ham, sliced
- 4 ounces cheese, sliced

Step-by-Step Directions to cook it:

1. Preheat the Cuisinart Convection Toaster Oven to 200^0C or 400^0F.
2. Apply olive oil and sprinkle oregano on both sides of bread slices.
3. Put the ham, spread cheese over one bread slice, and place the other on the sheet.
4. Bake for 10 minutes.

Nutritional value per serving:

Calories: 245kcal, Carbs: 28g, Protein: 16.18g, Fat: 18.53g.

Cheese Pizza

Enjoy weekends with this mouth-watering, easy, cheesy pizza recipe.

Prep Time and Cooking time: 20 minutes | Serves: 4

Ingredients to use:

- Readymade pizza base
- 2-3 tsp. tomato ketchup
- 100gm cheese, shredded
- Salt & pepper
- 2 ounces mushroom
- Capsicum, onions, tomatoes

Step-by-Step Directions to cook it:

1. Preheat the Cuisinart Convection Toaster Oven to 250^{0}C or 482^{0}F.
2. Spread ketchup on the pizza base and then toppings and cheese.
3. Bake for 10-12 minutes.

Nutritional value per serving:

Calories: 306kcal, Carbs: 40g, Protein: 15g, Fat: 11g.

Philly Cheesesteak Sandwiches

This sandwich is so satisfying and appetizing that no one would want to miss it.

Prep Time and Cooking time: 30 minutes | Serves: 6

Ingredients to use:

- 1-2 pounds steak
- 1 tsp. Worcestershire sauce
- Salt & pepper
- 2 tsp. butter
- 1 green bell pepper
- Cheese slices
- Bread rolls

Step-by-Step Directions to cook it:

1. Marinate the steak with sauce, pepper, and salt. Cook the steak in a pan with butter until brown.
2. Cook veggies for 2-3 mins
3. Slice steak and place it on bread rolls with veggies, sliced cheese, and bell peppers.
4. Bake for 15 minutes in the Cuisinart Convection Toaster Oven.

Nutritional value per serving:

Calories: 476kcal, Carbs: 15g, Protein: 37g, Fat: 35g.

Garlic Bread

With just these 4 simple ingredients, garlic bread can be prepared in minutes.

Prep Time and Cooking time: 20 minutes | Serves: 4

Ingredients to use:

- 4 pieces baguette, cut in half
- Mint leaves, chopped
- 2-3 tsp. butter
- 2-3 garlic cloves, minced

Step-by-Step Directions to cook it:

1. Mix butter, mint, and garlic.
2. Spread mixture on every slice.
3. Bake at 200C or 400F in the Cuisinart Convection Toaster Oven for 5-6 minutes

Nutritional value per serving:

Calories: 160kcal, Carbs: 18g, Protein: 3.6g, Fat: 7.1g.

Chicken Focaccia Bread Sandwiches

No need to grill up your pan to enjoy this meal. The toaster oven will do the trick!

Prep Time and Cooking time: 15 minutes | Serves: 6

Ingredients to use:

- Flatbread or Focaccia, halved
- 2 cups chicken, sliced
- Fresh basil leaves
- 1 cup sweet pepper, roasted

Step-by-Step Directions to cook it:

1. Roast the chicken at 177^0C or 350^0F in the Cuisinart Convection Toaster Oven for 25 to 30 minutes.
2. Spread mayonnaise on the bread and put the remaining ingredients on top.

Nutritional value per serving:

Calories: 263cal, Carbs: 26.9g, Protein: 19g, Fat: 10g.

Pepperoni Pizza

Make pepperoni pizza easily using a toaster oven with this savory recipe.

Prep Time and Cooking time: 30 minutes | Serves: 8

Ingredients to use:

- Pepperoni, sliced
- 1 cup pizza sauce
- 1 cup mozzarella cheese
- Readymade pizza dough
- Parmesan cheese, grated

Step-by-Step Directions to cook it:

1. Arrange toppings on pizza dough.
2. Preheat the Cuisinart Convection Toaster Oven to 177°C or 350°F.
3. Bake for 25 minutes.

Nutritional value per serving:

Calories: 235kcal, Carbs: 35.6g, Protein: 11g, Fat: 11g.

Chapter 8: Bagel and Waffle

Buttermilk Waffles

Transform your regular boring morning to a nutritious, toothsome one.

Prep time and cooking time: 20 minutes. | Serves: 5

Ingredients to use:

- 2 eggs
- 2 cups flour
- 2 tsp. sugar and vanilla extract
- 1 tsp. salt and baking soda
- 2 tsp. baking powder
- 2 cups buttermilk
- 1/2 cup butter

Step-by-Step Directions to cook it:

1. Whisk all the dry ingredients and then the wet ingredients in a bowl.
2. Preheat the Cuisinart Convection Toaster Oven at 150^0C or 300^0F and bake for 3-4 minutes.

Nutritional value per serving:

Calories: 423 kcal, Carbs: 43g, Protein: 9g, Fat: 23g.

Simple Bagel

A simple bagel recipe with just 5 additives.

Prep time and cooking time: 30 minutes. | Serves: 4

Ingredients to use:

- 1 cup flour
- 1 egg white, beaten
- 3 tsp. salt
- 2 tsp. baking powder
- 1 cup yogurt.

Step-by-Step Directions to cook it:

1. Add all the ingredients to make the dough.
2. Knead the dough until tacky.
3. Make small balls and roll to give a shape.
4. Sprinkle toppings if required.
5. Preheat the Cuisinart Convection Toaster Oven to 190°C or 375°F and bake for 20-25 minutes.

Nutritional value per serving:

Calories: 152cal, Carbs: 26.5g, Protein: 10g, Fat: 0.3g.

Brown Sugar Bacon Waffles

This is a light yet appetizing breakfast for daily mornings.

Prep time and cooking time: 40 minutes. | Serves: 7

Ingredients to use:

- 7 slices bacon
- 3 cups flour
- 1 tbsp. baking powder
- 1 tsp. baking soda and salt
- 1/2 cup brown sugar
- 4 eggs
- 2 tsp. vanilla extract
- 2/3 cup grapeseed oil
- 2 cups buttermilk

Step-by-Step Directions to cook it:

1. Mix all dry ingredients and then wet ingredients to make the batter.
2. Preheat the Cuisinart Convection Toaster Oven to 180^0C or 350^0F
3. Grease the waffle pan, pour the mix and bake for 15 minutes.

Nutritional value per serving:

Calories: 389kcal, Carbs: 76g, Protein: 18.4g, Fat: 23g.

Italian Waffle Cookies

Mornings will be brighter than ever before with these waffle cookies.

Prep time and cooking time: 30 minutes. | Serves: 4

Ingredients to use:

- 4 cups flour
- 1 cup butter
- 6 eggs
- 1 tsp. vanilla extract
- 1-1/2 cup sugar
- 1/4 tsp. salt

Step-by-Step Directions to cook it:

1. Beat the eggs until thick. Mix in melted butter.
2. Mix the remaining ingredients to make the batter.
3. Preheat the Cuisinart Convection Toaster Oven to 200°C or 400°F.
4. Bake the batter in a waffle pan for 15-18 minutes.

Nutritional value per serving:

Calories: 132kcal, Carbs: 17g, Protein: 2g, Fat: 5g.

Strawberry Ricotta Waffles

Waffles featuring fresh seasonal strawberry toppings for a healthy breakfast.

Prep time and cooking time: 20 minutes. | Serves: 2

Ingredients to use:

- 2 cups flour
- 1 tsp. baking soda, 2tsp baking powder
- 2 eggs
- 2 tbsp. sugar
- 1/2 tsp. vanilla extract
- 2 cups milk
- 1/4 cup oil
- 1/2 cup strawberries, sliced
- 1/4 cup ricotta cheese
- 2 tsp. maple syrup

Step-by-Step Directions to cook it:

1. Preheat the Cuisinart Convection Toaster Oven to 200^0C or 400^0F
2. Whisk the dry and wet batter ingredients.
3. Pour batter into the mold and bake for 12-15 minutes.
4. Mix ricotta and vanilla in a bowl. Top with the mixture, syrup, and strawberries.

Nutritional value per serving:

Calories: 318cal, Carbs: 43.1g, Protein: 11.9g, Fat: 13.6g.

Pineapple Bagel Brûlées

Treat your friends with the taste of this rich and tasty bagel.

Prep time and cooking time: 20 minutes. | Serves: 8

Ingredients to use:

- 4 thin bagels
- 4 tsp. brown sugar
- 3/4 cup low-fat cream cheese
- 8 slices pineapples
- 3 tbsp. almonds, toasted

Step-by-Step Directions to cook it:

1. Preheat the Cuisinart Convection Toaster Oven at 220°C or 425°F.
2. Bake the pineapple slices with brown sugar sprinkled on top.
3. Toast bagels, and apply cream cheese, almonds, and baked pineapples.

Nutritional value per serving:

Calories: 157cal, Carbs: 22.9g, Protein: 5.6g, Fat: 6.4g.

Golden Egg Bagels

A healthy yet light breakfast recipe in a convection oven.

Prep time and cooking time: 20 minutes. | Serves: 8

Ingredients to use:

- 2 eggs
- 4 tsp. dry yeast
- 4-5 cups all-purpose flour
- 1 tbsp. canola oil and kosher salt
- 1-1/2 tbsp. sugar

Step-by-Step Directions to cook it:

1. Whisk eggs, sugar, yeast, lukewarm, water, and oil. Add flour and salt to prepare the dough.
2. Make a long rope with the dough, locking both ends.
3. Preheat the Cuisinart Convection Toaster Oven to 200°C or 400°F.
4. Boil bagels in sugar and salt for 45 seconds.
5. Drain bagels, brush with egg white and bake for 15-20 mins.

Nutritional value per serving:

Calories: 164cal, Carbs: 28.4g, Protein: 6.6g, Fat: 2.1g.

Wild Blueberry Bagels

Make this breakfast meal in 5 minutes on a busy day.

Prep time and cooking time: 5minutes. | Serves: 1

Ingredients to use:

- 1 bagel
- 1 tbsp. low-fat cream cheese
- 2 tbsp. frozen wild blueberries
- 1/4 tsp. cinnamon

Step-by-Step Directions to cook it:

1. Preheat the Cuisinart Convection Toaster Oven to 190^{0}C or 375^{0}F
2. Toast the bagel for 3-5 minutes.
3. Spread cream cheese, add blueberry toppings, and cinnamon.

Nutritional value per serving:

Calories: 155cal, Carbs: 25g, Protein: 6g, Fat:3.5g.

Southwestern Waffles

With this tasty, wholesome recipe, you'll want waffles for lunch and dinner too!

Prep time and cooking time: 10minutes. | Serves: 1

Ingredients to use:

- 1 egg, fried
- 1/4 avocado, chopped
- 1 frozen waffle
- 1 tbsp. salsa

Step-by-Step Directions to cook it:

1. Preheat the Cuisinart Convection Toaster Oven to 200^{0}C or 400^{0}F.
2. Bake the waffles for 5-7 minutes.
3. Add avocado, fried eggs, and fresh salsa as toppings.

Nutritional value per serving:

Calories: 207cal, Carbs: 17g, Protein: 9g, Fat: 12g.

Pumpkin Spice Bagels

This pumpkin spice bagel is a quick and healthy breakfast.

Prep time and cooking time: 30minutes | Serves: 1

Ingredients to use:

- 1 egg
- 1 cup flour
- 1/2 tsp. pumpkin spice
- 1/2 cup Greek yogurt

Step-by-Step Directions to cook it:

1. Create a dough with flour, pie spice, yogurt, and pumpkin in a stand mixer.
2. Shape the dough into a few ropes and make bagels.
3. Apply egg and water mixture over the bagels.
4. Preheat the Cuisinart Convection Toaster Oven to 190°C or 375°F and bake for 20-25 minutes.

Nutritional value per serving:

Calories: 183, Carbs: 32.7g, Protein: 9.4g, Fat: 2g.

Chapter 9: Toasting and Baking Recipes

Lasagna Toast

Craving lasagna but don't want to spend much time in the kitchen? Lasagna toast can be a quick substitute then.

Prep and Cooking time: 30 minutes | Serves: 2

Ingredients to use:

- 4 slices bread
- 4 cherry tomatoes, chopped
- 1 small zucchini, chopped
- 1/2 cup cheddar cheese
- 1/2 cup mozzarella cheese
- 1 tbsp. olive oil
- 1 clove garlic

Step-by-step Directions to Cook it:

1. Preheat the Cuisinart Convection Toaster Oven to 200^{0}C or 400^{0}F.
2. Mix the veggies, spices, cheese, and oil in a bowl.
3. Spread the mixture all over the bread and top with another bread.
4. Toast it for 5 minutes.

Nutritional value per serving:

Calories: 250kcal, Carbs: 16g, Protein: 35g, Fat: 9g.

Strawberry Ricotta Toast

This hearty and insta-worthy breakfast will help you start the day right.

Prep and Cooking time: 10 minutes | Serves: 2

Ingredients to use:

- 2 slices of wheat bread
- 5 strawberries, chopped
- 100gm ricotta cheese
- 1 tbsp. ground cinnamon
- 2 eggs
- 2 tbsp. pistachios
- Honey

Step-by-step Directions to Cook it:

1. Whisk eggs with cinnamon in a bowl.
2. Soak the bread slices in the egg mixture.
3. Toast the bread in the preheated Cuisinart Convection Toaster Oven.
4. Spread ricotta, strawberries, and pistachios on the freshly toasted bread.
5. Drizzle some honey on top.

Nutritional value per serving:

Calories: 195kcal, Carbs: 10g, Protein: 15g, Fat: 4g.

Ham Avocado Toast

This amazing ham and avocado toast will definitely put you in a better mood.

Prep and Cooking time: 10 minutes | Serves: 2

Ingredients to use:

- 2 wheat bread, sliced
- 4 slices deli ham
- 1 ripe avocado
- 1/2 cup shredded cheese

Step-by-step Directions to Cook it:

1. Toast the bread in the Cuisinart Convection Toaster Oven until golden.
2. Mash the avocado and spread it on the bread along with two slices of ham.
3. Evenly sprinkle the shredded cheese on top.
4. Bake until the cheese melts.

Nutritional value per serving:

Calories: 155kcal, Carbs: 9g, Protein: 19g, Fat: 9g.

Tuna Melt Toastie

Start your day with this delicious tuna treat and we are pretty sure you won't regret it.

Prep and Cooking time: 15 minutes | Serves: 2

Ingredients to use:

- 150gm canned tuna
- 1/2 cup cilantro, chopped
- 2 slices wheat bread
- 3 tbsp. mayonnaise
- 50g mozzarella, grated
- Paprika.

Step-by-step Directions to Cook it:

1. Preheat the Cuisinart Convection Toaster Oven to 150°C or 300°F.
2. Mix all the ingredients except for bread.
3. Spread the tuna mixture on the bread and put the grated cheese on top.
4. Bake until the cheese melts.

Nutritional value per serving:

Calories: 613kcal, Carbs: 10g, Protein: 35g, Fat: 40g.

Pizza Toast

Try out the easiest recipe to satisfy your pizza cravings.

Prep and Cooking time: 5 minutes | Serves: 2

Ingredients to use:

- 4 slices bread.
- 1/2 cup grated mozzarella.
- Pepperoni
- 1/2 tbsp. Italian herbs.
- 1/2 cup marinara sauce

Step-by-step Directions to Cook it:

1. Spread marinara and grated cheese on the bread.
2. Put pepperoni and sprinkle some oregano.
3. Grill it in the preheated Cuisinart Convection Toaster Oven for 5 minutes.

Nutritional value per serving:

Calories: 175kcal, Carbs: 20g, Protein: 9g, Fat: 7g.

Baked Meatloaf

Here's an easy meatloaf recipe that is hard to resist.

Prep and Cooking time: 60 minutes | Serves: 4

Ingredients to use:

- 1 lb. ground beef
- 1 onion, chopped
- 1/2 cup tomato, diced
- 1 tbsp. Italian herbs
- 1 tbsp. paprika
- 1 egg
- Salt & pepper
- 1/2 tbsp. garlic, minced
- 2 tbsp. olive oil

Step-by-step Directions to Cook it:

1. Preheat the Cuisinart Convection Toaster Oven to 232°C or 450°F.
2. Combine all the ingredients in a bowl.
3. Grease a loaf pan with olive oil and put the mixture in it.
4. Bake it for 40 minutes.

Nutritional value per serving:

Calories: 195kcal, Protein: 56g, Fat: 15g.

Lamb Chops

Here's a quick and healthy recipe for all the avid lamb chops lovers out there.

Prep and Cooking time: 50 minutes | Serves: 4

Ingredients to use:

- 700gm lamb chops
- 1/3 cup olive oil
- 1 tbsp. garlic, minced
- 1/2 tbsp. oregano
- 2 tbsp. BBQ sauce
- 1 tbsp. soy sauce
- Salt & pepper
- 3 tbsp. lemon juice

Step-by-step Directions to Cook it:

1. Preheat the Cuisinart Convection Toaster Oven to 200⁰C or 400⁰F.
2. Mix all the ingredients in a pan.
3. Marinate the chops for 20 minutes with the mixture.
4. Bake it in the Cuisinart Convection Toaster Oven for 30 minutes
5. Let it for 5 minutes before serving.

Nutritional value per serving:

Calories: 294kcal, Protein: 25g, Fat: 21g.

Mediterranean Baked Fish

This delicate baked fish with a spicy kick will make your heart smile.

Prep and Cooking time: 20 minutes | Serves: 4

Ingredients to use:

- 4 white boneless fish fillets
- 1 large onion, diced
- 1 tomato, diced
- 1/2 tbsp. paprika
- 1/2 tbsp. cumin powder
- 1/2 tbsp. coriander powder
- 1 clove garlic, minced
- 3 tbsp. olive oil
- 1/3 cup lime juice
- 1/2 cup of water

Step-by-step Directions to Cook it:

1. Mix all the ingredients and marinate the fillets for 10 minutes.
2. Bake it in the Cuisinart Convection Toaster Oven for 10 minutes.
3. Serve with fresh cilantro on top.

Nutritional value per serving:

Calories: 170kcal, Protein: 14g, Fat: 35g.

Baked Cinnamon Apple

Check out this baked apple recipe to satisfy your sweet tooth in a healthy way.

Prep and Cooking time: 10 minutes | Serves: 3

Ingredients to use:

- 3 apples, cut
- 1/2 tbsp. ground cinnamon
- 1/2 tbsp. vanilla
- 1 tbsp. brown sugar

Step-by-step Directions to Cook it:

1. Preheat the Cuisinart Convection Toaster Oven to 120^0C or 250^0F.
2. Coat the apples with cinnamon, sugar, and vanilla.
3. Bake for 10 minutes. Serve with ice cream.

Nutritional value per serving:

Calories: 214kcal, Carbs: 36g, Protein: 0.4g, Fat: 0.9g.

Baked Chicken Stew

This comforting stew will put a smile on your face on a chilly winter day.

Prep and Cooking time: 35 minutes | Serves: 2

Ingredients to use:

- 1 cup boneless chicken, cut
- 1 large potato and 1 carrot, cut
- 1 stalk celery
- 1/2 tbsp. thyme
- 1 tbsp. flour
- 1 bay leaf
- 1 cup chicken stock
- Salt & pepper
- Cilantro, chopped

Step-by-step Directions to Cook it:

1. Add 2 tbsp. water in the flour to make a slurry.
2. Mix all the ingredients in a bowl.
3. Cook it in the Cuisinart Convection Toaster Oven with a foil lining.
4. Serve with fresh cilantro on top.

Nutritional value per serving:

Calories: 237kcal, Carbs: 42g, Protein: 30g, Fat: 15g.

Chapter 10: Roasting Recipes

Miso Glazed Salmon

Check out one of the quickest, easiest, and least messy ways to cook glazed salmon.

Prep and Cooking time: 15 minutes | Serves: 4

Ingredients to use:

- 4 salmon filets
- 1/4 cup miso
- 1/3 cup sugar
- 1 tsp. soy sauce
- 1/3 cup sake
- 2 tsp. vegetable oil

Step-by-step Directions to Cook it:

1. Whisk all the ingredients, except for filets, in a bowl.
2. Marinate the filets with the mixture for 10 minutes.
3. Preheat the Cuisinart Convection Toaster Oven to high and roast it for 5 minutes.

Nutritional value per serving:

Calories: 331.8kcal, Carbs: 2gProtein: 34 g, Fat: 17.9 g.

Fireless S'mores

Get this perfect summer dessert all year round without having to place a campfire!

Prep and Cooking time: 5 minutes | Serves: 4

Ingredients to Use:

- 8 graham crackers
- 4 marshmallows
- 1 dark chocolate bar, chopped

Step-by-step Directions to Cook it:

1. Put all the ingredients on top of the graham cracker and top with another cracker.
2. Roast it in the Cuisinart Convection Toaster Oven for 2 minutes.

Nutritional value per serving:

Calories: 87kcal, Carbs: 6g, Protein: 01g, Fat: 03 g.

Slow Roasted Herb Chicken

If you want your chicken dinner to be both healthy and yummy, this recipe is here to pack the punch.

Prep and Cooking time: 60 minutes | Serves: 4

- 1 lb. whole chicken
- 1 tbsp. rosemary
- 1 tbsp. basil
- 1 tbsp. thyme
- 1/2 tsp. salt
- 1 tbsp. garlic, minced
- 1/2 tsp. pepper
- 1 tbsp. olive oil
- 1 lemon

Step-by-step Directions to Cook it:

1. Mix all the dry ingredients, garlic, and oil in a bowl.
2. Rub the mixture on the chicken and stuff some lemon inside the chicken.
3. Roast the chicken for 40 minutes in a preheated Cuisinart Convection Toaster Oven.

Nutritional value per serving:

Calories⌐: ⌐127kcal, Protein: 26.3 g, Fat: 0.5 g.

Standing Rib Roast

This classic and comforting holiday meal is beyond any description.

Prep and Cooking time: 90 minutes | Serves: 8

Ingredients to Use:

- 5 lb. rib-eye meat
- Salt & pepper
- 1 tbsp. thyme
- 1 tbsp. rosemary
- 1 stick unsalted butter

Step-by-step Directions to Cook it:

1. Preheat the Cuisinart Convection Toaster Oven to 230°C or 450°F.
2. Mix the butter and dry ingredients in a bowl.
3. Rub the mixture on the rib and roast it for an hour in the preheated oven.
4. Serve with fresh herbs on top.

Nutritional value per serving:

Calories: 185kcal, Protein: 52.0 g, Fat: 48 g.

Chicken Breast with Veggies

No matter what time of the year it is, this classic chicken dish in dinner can never go wrong.

Prep and Cooking time: 50 minutes | Serves: 4

Ingredients to use:

- 4 deboned chicken breasts
- 1 tbsp. dried Italian herbs
- Salt & pepper
- 1 tbsp. paprika
- 1 large carrot, chopped
- 1 large potato, chopped

Step-by-step Directions to Cook it:

1. Preheat the Cuisinart Convection Toaster Oven to 150⁰C or 300⁰F.
2. Mix all the seasonings and coat the chicken and veggies.
3. Roast the chicken and veggies for 30 minutes.

Nutritional value per serving:

Calories⌐: ⌐140kcal, Protein: 22.3 g, Fat: 0.5 g.

Roasted Spaghetti Squash

Here's something healthy to munch on that won't take up a lot of time to make.

Prep and Cooking time: 30 minutes | Serves: 4

Ingredients to use:

- 1 ripe squash
- Salt & pepper

Step-by-step Directions to Cook it:

1. Preheat the Cuisinart Convection Toaster Oven to 150^0C or 300^0F.
2. Prick the outside of the cleaned squash with a fork.
3. Roast it for 10 minutes.
4. Cut the roasted squash and scrape out the strands.
5. Sprinkle salt and pepper and serve.

Nutritional value per serving:

Calories: 42kcal, Carbs: 3g, Protein: 1g, Fat: 0.5g,

Roasted Filet Mignon

Check out this classic steak recipe if you want to bring back the 90's vibe in your dinner table.

Prep and Cooking time: 30 minutes | Serves: 2

Ingredients to use:

- 10 ounces filet mignon
- 1 tbsp. Italian herbs, chopped
- Salt & pepper
- 2 tbsp. olive oil

Step-by-step Directions to Cook it:

1. Preheat the Cuisinart Convection Toaster Oven to 200⁰C or 400⁰F.
2. Mix all the seasonings and oil, and rub the mixture on the steak.
3. Roast it for 30 minutes.

Nutritional value per serving:

Calories: 267kcal, Protein: 26g, Fat: 17g

Roasted Pears

Here's a healthy roasted fruit recipe that'll make your mouth drool!

Prep and Cooking time: 60 minutes | Serves: 3

Ingredients to use:

- 3 semi-ripe pears
- 1/2 cup icing sugar
- 2 tbsp. butter
- 1 tbsp. ground cinnamon
- 3/4 cup white wine

Step-by-step Directions to Cook it:

1. Mix all the ingredients, except for pears.
2. Prick the pears with a fork and let it soak in the wine mixture for 15 minutes.
3. Roast in the preheated Cuisinart Convection Toaster Oven for 20 minutes.

Nutritional value per serving:

Calories: 103kcal, Carbs: 27g, Protein: 1g, Fat: 4g

Roasted Italian Sausage

Here's a quick and yummy meal prep recipe for the people who are always on the go.

Prep and Cooking time: 30 minutes | Serves: 4

Ingredients to use:

- 4 Italian sausage
- 1 large potato, chopped
- 2 ounces mushroom, chopped
- 1tbsp Italian herbs
- 1 tbsp. paprika
- Salt
- 1 clove garlic
- 2 tbsp. olive oil

Step-by-step Directions to Cook it:

1. Mix the seasonings and oil in a pan and coat the sausages and veggies.
2. Roast in the Cuisinart Convection Toaster Oven for 20 minutes.

Nutritional value per serving:

Calories: 81kcal, Carbs: 60g, Protein: 4.7g, Fat: 7g

Roasted Vegetable Pasta

This hearty and easy pasta recipe will help you save your time and fill your tummy.

Prep and Cooking time: 30 minutes | Serves: 4

Ingredients to use:

- 10-ounce linguine pasta
- 1/2 cup cilantro, chopped
- 5 cherry tomatoes, chopped
- 1 zucchini, chopped
- 1/2 cup marinara sauce
- Salt & pepper
- 1/2 cup parmesan cheese
- 2 tbsp. olive oil

Step-by-step Directions to Cook it:

1. Preheat the Cuisinart Convection Toaster Oven to 150°C or 300°F.
2. Stir in the veggies, pasta, and spices in a bowl with some water.
3. Roast for 20 minutes.
4. Sprinkle parmesan cheese on top.

Nutritional value per serving:

Calories: 179kcal, carbs: 40g, Protein: 6.3g, Fat: 1.5g

Conclusion

The recipes in this book should give you a head start in using your toaster oven and experimenting with your signature dishes. Now, head to a grocery store, buy all the ingredients that you'll need, and start making your favorite dish!

And remember, *you should eat not only to fill your stomach but to experience something new!*

CPSIA information can be obtained
at www.ICGtesting.com
Printed in the USA
BVHW060734040222
627987BV00004B/170

9 781954 294172